Nita Mehta's
MORE
PANEER

Nita Mehta

B.Sc. (Home Science), M.Sc. (Food and Nutrition), Gold Medalist

GW00640734

Nita Mehta's
MORE
PANEER

© Copyright 1995-2002 **SNAB** Publishers Pvt Ltd

WORLD RIGHTS RESERVED. The contents—all recipes, photographs and drawings are original and copyrighted. No portion of this book shall be reproduced, stored in a retrieval system or transmitted by any means, electronic, mechanical, photocopying, recording or otherwise, without the written permission of the publishers.

While every precaution is taken in the preparation of this book, the publisher and the author assume no responsibility for errors or omissions. Neither is any liability assumed for damages resulting from the use of information contained herein.

TRADEMARKS ACKNOWLEDGED. Trademarks used, if any, are acknowledged as trademarks of their respective owners. These are used as reference only and no trademark infringement is intended upon.

10th Print 2002
ISBN 81-86004-09-2

Food Styling and Photography: **SNAB**

Layout and laser typesetting :

National Information Technology Academy
N.I.T.A.
☎ 3252948
3A/3, Asaf Ali Road
New Delhi-110002

Published by :

SNAB
Publishers Pvt. Ltd.
3A/3 Asaf Ali Road,
New Delhi - 110002
Tel: 3252948, 3250091
Telefax:91-11-3250091

Editorial and Marketing office:
E-348, Greater Kailash-II, N.Delhi-48
*Fax:*91-11-6235218 *Tel:*91-11-6214011, 6238727
E-Mail: nitamehta@email.com
          snab@snabindia.com
*Website:*http://www.nitamehta.com
Website: http://www.snabindia.com

Distributed by :

THE VARIETY BOOK DEPOT
A.V.G. Bhavan, M 3 Con Circus,
New Delhi - 110 001
Tel : 3327175, 3322567; Fax : 3714335

Printed by :

THOMSON PRESS (INDIA) LIMITED

Rs. 89/-

FOREWORD

My experiments with Paneer continue due to the exceeding demands of my son. A genuine lover of Paneer!

My experiments have brought out some exciting new recipes to add on to what you got in Book I. These recipes would further enliven your meal time environment.

Last though not the least, I wish to thank all my readers for their great enthusiasm & encouragement in inspiring me to write this second volume on Paneer.

I am grateful to my dear husband Subhash & my kids, Bhavna & Anurag for their cooperation and support.

Nita Mehita

With love to my dear son
Anurag
A genuine lover of Paneer!

CONTENTS

Indian Name	English Name
Achaar	Pickle
Ajwain	Omum, Carom seeds
Aloo	Potato
Amchoor	Dried mango powder
Anaar	Pomegranate
Anaardaana	Pomegranate seeds
Atta	Whole wheat flour
Badaam	Almonds
Besan	Gram flour
Bhutta	Corn cobs
Channa	Bengal gram
Channe ki dal	Split gram
Dahi	Yoghurt
Dalchini	Cinnamon
Dhania	Coriander
Dhania saboot	Coriander seeds

Indian Name	English Name
Garam masala	Mixed spices
Gobi	Cauliflower
Haldi	Turmeric
Hing	Asafoetida
Chhoti illaichi	Green cardamom
Imli	Tamarind
Kaju	Cashew nut
Kala-namak	Black salt, Rock salt
Kali mirch	Black pepper
Kali mirch saboot	Pepper corns
Kalonji	Nigella seeds, Onion seeds
Karela	Bitter gourd
Kasoori methi	Dry fenugreek leaves
Kesar	Saffron
Kheera	Cucumber
Khoya	Dried whole milk
Kishmish	Raisins

Indian Name	English Name
Laung	Cloves
Lehson	Garlic
Magaz	skinned seeds of cucumber, melon, water melon and pumpkin mixed together
Maida	Plain flour
Malai	Milk topping
Masoor ki dal	Lentil
Matar	Peas
Methi daana	Fenugreek seeds
Methi saag	Fenugreek leaves
Mooli	Radish
Moong ki dal	Split green gram
Moti illaichi	Brown cardamom
Nariyal	Coconut
Nariyal ka burada	Desiccated coconut
Palak	Spinach

Indian Name	English Name
Paneer	Cottage cheese
Pista	Pistachio
Poodina	Mint leaves
Rajmah	Kidney beans
Rai	Fine mustard seeds
Sabzi	Vegetable
Saunf	Aniseed
Seviyan	Vermicelli
Sirka	Vinegar
Suji	Semolina
Tej patta	Bay leaf
Til	Sesame seeds
Jeera	Cumin seeds
Jeera-bhuna	Roasted cumin seeds

Kitchen's Equipment

Indian Name   English Name

Indian Name	English Name
Pateela	Pots.
Karahi or kadhai	Deep frying pan with handles like a Chinese wok.
Karchhi	A laddle used for stirring.
Tawa	Griddle.
Chekla-Belan	Chakla is the round marble or wooden platform. Belan is the rolling pin.
Chimta	Tong.
Paraat	A utensil in which dough is kneaded.
Pauni	Perforated frying spoon.

HOW TO PREPARE PANEER

Paneer is readily available in the market, but due to shortage of milk in summers, paneer becomes scarce in certain parts of our country.

To make home made paneer, it is important to use good quality milk. Paneer prepared from full cream milk is certainly softer and tastier than that made from skimmed milk available at mother diary booths.

To make paneer at home, take out juice of one lemon in a small bowl, carefully removing the seeds. The seeds taste bitter if they come in the paneer by mistake. If there is no lemon, keep one cup of curd ready.

Boil one kg. of full cream milk, stirring continuously to prevent skin forming at the top. When it comes to boil, put off the fire. Add lemon juice or curd. Return to low heat, stir gently, till all the milk curdles and the greenish water called whey separates. Remove from fire. Leave it covered for 15 minutes. Strain through a muslin cloth and squeeze out all the whey.

If cubes of paneer are required, keep the paneer which is wrapped in the muslin cloth in a rectangular ice cream box or an aluminium ice tray. The paneer takes its shape. To get a compact brick of paneer, place a heavy weight on the paneer for an hour or so. Remove the cloth and use the perfect home made paneer even when it is not available in the market.

TIPS FOR PERFECTION

1. Always add hot water to the gravy. It will enhance the flavour of the dish.
2. Whenever curd is to be added to the masala, it should be beaten well with a spoon to make it smooth. It should then be added gradually to the masala, stirring continuously. The curd should be stirred on fire, till it turns brown and no longer remains white.
3. Paneer should be heated thoroughly at serving time, because only on heating properly, the paneer pieces turn soft. So at the time of serving, the paneer pieces in masala should be kept on slow fire, simmering, till they are heated through and become soft. Dry paneer preparations should be sprinkled with a little water when they are being heated for serving. This makes the paneer soft.
4. 2-3 days old paneer may not appear hard, but usually when the paneer is stale, the softness of paneer lessens.
5. When you prepare paneer at home, do not squeeze out the water completely. This makes the paneer taste dry.

6. The greenish liquid (whey) left after straining the home made paneer, should be used instead of water in your gravies. Being rich in nutrition, it should not be thrown.

7. If you are making a dry preparation of paneer, use the whey (greenish liquid) in kneading the dough for chappatis.

8. If by mistake, there is extra salt in your gravy, add a few drops of lemon juice to the gravy.

9. To prevent discolouring of vegetables like potatoes, brinjals, etc, keep putting them in salted water while cutting & leave them immersed in it.

10. Saffron should be soaked in a little warm milk or water for 5-7 minutes before use, for proper colour and flavour.

11. Ready made tomato puree can be substituted with fresh tomatoes or vice-versa. 1 medium fresh tomato = 1½ tbsp ready made tomato puree.

12. When paneer needs to be deep fried, it should never be put in oil which is not heated properly. It will stick to the karahi.

Handi Paneer : page 28

Paneer as a Garnish

Last, but not the least, a dash of paneer here and there, enhances the taste and appearance of food. Paneer garnishes the food appetizingly.

Grated or diced (tiny cubes) paneer, when added to soups like tomato, vegetable or even hot n' sour, changes it for the better.

A simple mixed vegetable preparation can look exotic with a sprinkling of finely grated paneer. The white paneer enhances the colourful looks of the vegetables.

A simple bhatura, when filled with a spicy paneer filling, just a tablespoon - turns it into a special one.

The rest, I leave to your imagination.

Stuffed Tomatoes in Gravy : page 42

Indian
Masala Mixes

5 gm = 1 tsp
15 gm = 1 tbsp

GARAM MASALA

INGREDIENTS

1 cup saboot dhania (coriander seeds)
5-6 long sticks dalchini (cinnamon)
15-20 moti illaichi (brown cardamom)
3/4 tbsp laung (cloves)
2 tbsp saboot kali mirch (black pepper corns)
½ cup jeera (cumin seeds)
½ flower of javetri (mace)

METHOD

1. Remove seeds of moti illaichi. Discard skin.
2. Roast all ingredients together on a tawa for 2 minutes on low flame, stirring constantly.
3. Remove from fire. Cool. Grind to a fine powder and keep tightly bottled.

CHAT MASALA/DAHI MASALA

(100 gm)

INGREDIENTS
40 gm jeera (cumin seeds)
40 gm dhania (coriander) powder
10 gm garam masala (powder)
10 gm amchoor (dried mango) powder
25 gm kala namak (black salt) powder
5 gms salt

METHOD
1. Roast jeera on a tawa or in a karahi to a golden brown colour.
2. Roast powdered dhania to a golden colour, add garam masala and roast lightly.
3. Powder roasted jeera finely and mix with other masalas.

KASHMIRI MASALA

(1.5 Kg)

INGREDIENTS

100 gm dhuli urad (black gram split) powder
100 gm dhania (coriander) powder
100 gm haldi (turmeric)
100 gm dry ginger powder
100 gm salt
15 gm kala jeera (black cumin seeds) powder
30 gm sufeed jeera (white cumin seeds) powder
25 laung (cloves) powdered
100 gm saunf (aniseeds) powder
100 gm garam masala
100 gm red chillies
50 gm hing (asafoetida)
30 ml water
350 ml sarson ka tel (mustard oil)

METHOD

1. Soak hing.
2. Mix all dry ingredients and mix with hing water and oil to make a dough.
3. Make about 12, small, circular, flat tikkis . Dry in sun and store.
4. Break a small piece and use as powder.

RASAM POWDER

(100 gm)

INGREDIENTS
55 gm saboot dhania (coriander seeds)
10 gm arhar (red gram) dal
20 gm saboot kali mirch (pepper corns)
5 gm whole dry red chillies
2 gm hing (asafoetida)
10 gm jeera (cumin seeds)

METHOD
Grind everything together in a raw form.

SAMBAR POWDER

(100 gm)

INGREDIENTS

50 gm saboot dhania (coriander seeds)
15 gm channe ki dal (split Bengal gram)
15 gm saboot kali mirch (pepper corns)
5 gm methi dana (fenugreek seeds)
10 gm dry whole red chillies
2 gm hing (asafoetida)
5 gm oil

METHOD

1. Fry or roast fenugreek seeds to a dark brown colour.
2. Fry all other ingredients and dry or wet grind as desired.
3. If desired, 25 gms fresh coconut can be grated and added to the other ingredients at the time of frying. It can be fried and ground with the masala wherever it is to be used.

Gravies & Curries

HAANDI PANEER

Picture on page 17

— Serves 4 —

Paneer 200 gms - cut into 1" cubes

MASALA
3 onions - very finely sliced
2" long , ginger piece - grated thickly into long shreds
1 green chilli - slit lengthways
1 tbsp chopped fresh dhania (coriander)
1 tomato - very finely chopped
1 tej patta (bay leaf)
½ cup curd - beaten
½ tsp haldi
½ tsp red chilli pd.
salt to taste

Pic. Page 17

½ tsp garam masala
5-6 saboot kali mirch (pepper corns)
4 tbsp oil

1. Cut onions into 2 halves. Then slice very finely.
2. Heat oil. Add onions. Stir-fry till onions turn brown.
3. Reduce flame. Add grated ginger. Stir. Add haldi, red chilli pd. & garam masala. Mix.
4. Add tomato, green chillies & tej patta. Cook for 7-8 minutes on low flame.
5. Beat the curd with a spoon till smooth. Add curd gradually. Cook for 2-3 minutes till dry. Add salt.
6. Add ½ cup water. Boil. Add paneer & coriander leaves. Cook on low flame till masala dries up a little and coats the paneer pieces.
7. Crush saboot kali mirch (frehly ground pepper) to a powder and add to the paneer. Remove from fire.
8. You may serve it in a small copper handi to make it look more appetizing. Garnish with slit green chillies.

PANEER MAKHANWAALA

Picture on page 35

— Serves 4 —

250 gms paneer - cut into 1" cubes & deep fried
4 tbsp oil
3 onions
1" ginger
3-4 flakes garlic
3 tbsp ready made tomato puree (Godrej's puree)
½ tsp haldi
1 tsp red chilli powder
1 tsp garama masala
3/4 tsp salt - to taste
4 tbsp (50 gm) fresh malai or cream
1½ tbsp butter - salted
2 tbsp kasoori methi (dried fenugreek leaves)
¼ - ½ tsp sugar

Pic Page 35

1. Deep fry big paneer pieces to a nice reddish brown colour. Keep aside.
2. To prepare gravy, grind onions, ginger & garlic to a paste in a grinder.
3. Fry onion paste in oil, on low flame, till golden.
4. Add haldi, red chilli pd, garam masala. Cook for ½ minute.
5. Add ready made tomato puree. Cook for 1 minute.
6. Add 2 cups water. Boil. Add sugar. Simmer on low flame for 7-8 minutes.
7. Add cream. Mix well.
8. Add butter & kasoori methi. Mix. Add salt to taste (3/4 tsp approx.).
9. Add fried paneer. Give one boil. Simmer on low flame for a few seconds till paneer turns soft.
10. Remove from fire. Serve.

Note : ¼ cup milk may be added instead of cream. Boil the gravy on high flame after adding milk for 5 minutes till thick.

Paneer Shahi Masala

— Serves 4 —

250 paneer - cut into 1" pieces
2 big onions - sliced
4 tomatoes
2" piece ginger - chopped
3 tsp magaz - tarbooz ke beej (water melon seeds)
2 tsp broken kaju (cashew nuts)
1 tsp red chilli powder
½ tsp dhania (coriander)powder
½ tsp garam masala
3 tbsp oil or ghee
4 laung (cloves) - crushed
1½ tsp salt or to taste

1. Soak magaz & kaju in ¼ cup water.
2. Deep fry paneer to a light colour in hot oil.
3. Deep fry sliced onions to a light brown colour. Remove from oil.
4. Grind the fried onions to a paste. Keep onion paste aside.
5. Cut each tomato into 4 big pieces. Boil tomatoes with ginger in 3/4 cup water. Cook tomatoes till the water is almost dry and they turn soft.
6. Cool tomatoes. Grind to a puree. Keep aside.
7. Grind the soaked kaju & magaz to a paste. If the mixture is too little to be ground in an electric grinder, add some onion paste.
8. Heat 2 tbsp ghee or 4 tbsp oil.
9. Add onion paste & cook for 2-3 minutes on low flame to a golden brown colour.
10. Add kaju-magaz paste & cook for 1 minute.
11. Add red chilli pd, dhania pd & garam masala. Stir for 1 minute.
12. Add the tomato puree & cook for 5-7 minutes, till oil separates
13. Add 1 cup hot water. Boil. Keep boiling on low flame for 10 minutes.
14. Add ssalt, crushed laung & fried paneer.
15. Simmer for a few minutes. Serve hot.

PANEER DO PYAZA

— Serves 4 —

150 gms paneer - cut into finger shaped pieces
2 big onions - cut into slices
4 tbsp chopped fresh dhania (coriander)
1 firm tomato - cut into 1" pieces
1 green chilli - finely cut lengthways
1/2 " piece ginger - cut into long shreds
2 tbsp oil
1½ tsp crushed saboot dhania (coriander seeds)
½ tsp salt
¼ tsp garam masala
¼ tsp red chilli pd.

GRAVY
3 onions

Paneer Makhanwaala : page 30

1" piece ginger
½ cup curd
5 tbsp oil
2 sticks dalchini (cinnamon)
¼ tsp haldi
½ tsp salt
½ tsp red chilli pd
½ tsp garam masala
1 tsp dhania (coriander) pd.
seeds of 2 moti illiachi (big cardamom)

1. Cut tomato into half. Cut each half into 4 equal pieces. Remove pulp & keep pieces aside.
2. Slice onions. Slit green chillies, deseed, & cut into long thin pieces.
3. Crush saboot dhania on a chakla belan to a rough powder. Keep aside.
4. Heat 2 tbsp oil. Add sliced onions & stir-fry till they start turning brown. Add crushed dhania. cook for 1 minute on low flame.

Stuffed Paneer : page 86

5. Add garam masala & chilli pd. Mix well.
6. Add tomato pieces, green chilli, ginger and paneer.
7. Sprinkle hara dhania on the paneer. Mix gently. Stir for 1-2 minutes on low flame. Keep aside.
8. To prepare the gravy, grind 3 onions & 1" piece ginger together.
9. In a clean karahi, heat 5 tbsp oil. Add dalchini. After ½ minute, add the onion paste. Stir fry till onions turn golden brown.
10. Add salt, haldi, dhania pd, red chilli pd. & garam masala. Cook for a few seconds. Add the tomato pulp & cook for 2-3 minutes.
11. Beat curd with a spoon & add it gradually to the onion paste.
12. Cook for 10-15 minutes till the masala turns brown again & the oil separates.
13. Cursh seeds of moti illiachi on chakla - belan & add to the masala. Cook for a few seconds.
14. Add enough hot water, about 1 cup, to get a thick masala gravy. Boil gravy. Simmer on low heat for 5 minutes.
15. Add the pyaz - paneer mixture prepared earlier. Mix gently. Remove from fire.

Mughlai Kofta

250 gms paneer is required in all.

COVERING
200 gm paneer
2 tbsp maida (plain flour)
¼ tsp garam masala
½ tsp salt
¼ tsp red chilli powder

FILLING
1 tbsp oil
1 onion - very finely chopped
50 gms paneer
1 green chilli - finely chopped
1 tbsp finely chopped fresh dhania (coriander)
¼" piece ginger - grated

10 badam (almonds)- finely chopped
¼ tsp salt, ¼ red chilli pd.

GRAVY
½ kg (6 big) onions - sliced finely
10-12 kaju (cashewnuts)
1 tbsp khus-khus (poppy seeds)
¼ cup fresh curd
2 tomatoes - blanched & pureed
½ cup milk
½ cup water (approx)
4 tbsp, 2 tbsp oil (6 tbsp)
1 tsp salt - to taste
3/4 tsp red chilli powder
¼ tsp garam masala (mixed spices)

1. Mash 50 gms paneer roughly (crumble) with the fingers.
2. Heat 1 tbsp oil. Fry the chopped onion to a light brown colour.
3. Add curmbled paneer and all other ingredients of the filling. Mix well.

Remove from fire. Keep the filling aside.

4. To prepare the covering, grate 200 gms of paneer.
5. Knead the grated paneer with the palms well, till the grains disappear.
6. Add maida and all spices of the covering. Mix well & knead some more. Divide into 12 portions. Make balls.
7. Flatten each ball and put 1 tsp of filling in each. Shape into balls again. Deep fry on medium fire to a golden brown colour. Keep koftas aside.
8. To prepare gravy, heat 4 tbsp oil and fry onions, kaju & khus-khus till onions turn golden brown. Remove from fire. Grind to a wet paste with ¼ cup water.
9. Peel tomatoes by putting in boiling water for 2-3 minutes. Grind the blanched (peeled) tomatoes to a puree.
10. Heat 2 tbsp oil. Add the onion paste and cook on low heat till golden brown in colour. Add beaten curd. Cook till the paste turns brown again. Add pureed tomatoes. Cook on low flame, till oil separates.
11. Add milk and enough water to get a thick gravy. Add salt, pepper, red chilli pd. & garam masala. Boil the gravy and simmer for 3-4 minutes.
12. Put the koftas in hot gravy at the time of serving & heat for a few seconds

Stuffed Tomatoes in Gravy

Picture on page 18

— Serves 4 —

4 medium sized firm tomatoes
2-3 tbsp oil

FILLING

150 gms (1½ cups) paneer - crumbled
2-3 tbsp chopped coriander
2 green chillies
1 tsp chaat masala
½ tsp salt or to taste
½ tsp garam masala
½ tsp red chilli powder

GRAVY

2 big onions
1" piece ginger

¼ cup curd
½ tsp haldi
1 tsp dhania (coriander) powder
½ tsp red chilli pd.
3/4 tsp salt - to taste
½ tsp garam masala
2 tbsp chopped fressh dhania (coriander)

1. Slice a small piece from the top of each tomato. Scoop out carefully, keeping the scooped tomato aside for the gravy.
2. Rub a little salt on the inside of the tomatoes & keep them upside down for 10 minutes.
3. Mash paneer roughly (crumble). Add all other ingredients of the filling and mix lightly. Do not mash.
4. Fill the scooped tomatoes with the filling. Press well. Keep the left over filling (2 tbsp) aside for the gravy.
5. Heat 2-3 tbsp oil in a karahi & gently put the stuffed tomatoes in it. Cover & cook on low flame for 4-5 minutes till tomatoes become a little

soft. Gently keep turning the tomatoes occasionally & take care not to discolour them. Remove from oil. Alternately, rub a little oil over the tomatoes and bake in a moderately hot oven for 8-10 minutes. Do not let thembe in the oven for a longer period, otherwise they will turn limp. Keep aside.

6. To prepare the gravy, grind onions, ginger and the scooped out portion of the tomatoes, together in a blender.
7. Heat 3-4 tbsp oil. Add the onion-tomato paste & cook till oil separates.
8. Beat curd lightly with a spoon & add gradually.
9. Cook on low flame till the masala turns brown again.
10. Add haldi, dhania powder, red chili pd, salt & garam masala. Cook for 1 minute.
11. Add 1½ cups hot water to get a thick gravy. Boil. Simmer on low flame for 7-8 minutes.
12. Add the left over paneer of the filling (2 tbsp) & fresh coriander. Mix well. Remove from fire. Keep aside.
13. To serve, boil gravy. Add stuffed tomatoes gently. **Cover** & simmer for 5-6 minutes, on very low flame, till the filling also gets heated.

Paneer Balls in Paalak Gravy

— Serves 8 —

BALLS
100 gm paneer
1 slice bread
1 tbsp curd
¼ tsp roasted jeera (cumin seeds) powder
¼ tsp red chilli pd
¼ tsp salt
2 tbsp maida (plain flour) - to coat

GRAVY
250 gm paalak (spinach)
2 green chillies
2 onions - grated
3 tbsp ready-made tomato puree (Godrej's puree)
OR
2 tomatoes - pureed in a blender

1" piece ginger - crushed to a paste
5-7 flakes garlic (optional) - crushed to a paste
3 tbsp desi ghee or 4 tbsp oil
½ tsp haldi powder
½ tsp garam masala
½ tsp red chilli powder
salt to taste
a pinch of sugar - optional

1. Remove sides of bread. Spread 1 tbsp of curd on the slice. Keep aside for 5 minutes.
2. Grate paneer. Mash bread. Mix paneer, bread, jeera powder, red chilli powder and salt.
3. Make 8 marble sized balls. Roll in dry maida & deep fry to a golden brown colour. Keep aside.
4. Discard stems of palak leaves. Wash leaves in lots of water to remove grains of sand or soil. Pressure cook with ¼ cup water to give one whistle. Keep on low flame for 5-7 minutes. Remove from fire. Cool. Grind along with green chillies in a mixer.

5. Heat ghee & fry onions to a golden colour.
6. Add tomato puree & cook on low flame for 1 minute. If puree of fresh tomatoes is used, cook for 3-4 minutes on low flame till puree dries up a little and the ghee separates.
7. Crush ginger and garlic on a chakla-belan and add to the masala. Cook for ½ minute.
8. Add ½ tsp each of salt, haldi, garam masala & red chilli powder.
9. Add paalak & cook for 1 minute.
10. Add 1½ cups hot water to get a thin green gravy. Boil. Keep on low flame for 10-15 minutes. Add a pinch of sugar if desired.
11. At serving time, add paneer balls. Keep on low flame for 2-3 minutes. Serve hot with tandoori paranthas.

My Special Matar Paneer

— Serves 4 —

150 gms paneer - cut into 1" cubes
3/4 cup shelled peas

GRAVY

3 onions - sliced finely
3 tomatoes - chopped
3 flakes garlic - crushed (optional)
1" piece ginger - chopped
3 tsp magaz - tarbooz ke beej (watermelon seeds)
1 tsp khus khus (poppy seeds)
1 tsp salt
½ tsp red chilli pd.
½ tsp garam masala
½ cup milk

1. Deep fry paneer cubes to a golden colour. Keep aside.
2. In the same oil, deep fry sliced onions to a golden brown colour. Remove from oil. Cool. Grind to a paste with very little water.
3. Mix tomatoes, garlic, ginger with 1 cup water in a small pan. Boil. Keep covered on low flame for 15 minutes till the tomatoes turn soft. Remove from fire. Cool. Grind to a puree. Keep puree aside.
4. Soak magaz & khus khus in ¼ cup water for 10 minutes. Grind to a paste. If the quantity is too little for grinding in an electric grinder, add 2-3 tbsp of the above onion paste.
5. Heat 2 tbsp oil. Add onion paste. Fry till golden brown.
6. Add red chilli pd. Add khus khus paste. Stir for a few seconds.
7. Add tomato puree. Cook for 5-7 minutes till oil separates.
8. Add milk gradually, stirring continuously for 2 minutes on low flame.
9. Add garam masala & salt to taste. Add shelled peas. Fry for 2-3 minutes.
10. Add enough hot water to get a thick gravy. Cook covered till peas are done or transfer to a presssure cooker and give one whistle.
11. Add the fried paneer. Give one boil. Simmer on low flame for 3-4 minutes till the paneer is heated through & turns soft. Serve.

Nargasi Kofta

Picture on page 54

— Serves 8 —

KOFTAS

75 gms paneer - grated
few strands of kesar (saffron) or yellow colour
250 gm bhein or kamal kakri (lotus stem)
2 green chillies - finely chopped
1 tsp grated ginger
salt & pepper to taste
1 tsp jeera (cumin seeds) - powdered
2 slices bread - squeezed out of water
2 chhoti illaichi (green cardamom)

GRAVY

3 onions
2 flakes garlic - (optional)
1 " piece ginger

3 tomatoes
½ tsp jeera (cumin seeds) - powdered
½ tsp garam masala
½ tsp red chilli powder
salt to taste
a small pinch amchoor (dried mango powder)
1 laung (clove)
3 chhoti illaichi (green cardamoms)
4 tbsp oil

1. Peel, scrape bhei. Cut into 3" long pieces. Pressure cook in salted water to give one whistle. Keep on low flame for 15-20 minutes.
2. Strain, cool & mash bhei. Mix grated ginger, wet bread pieces, green chillies, salt & pepper to taste.
4. Crush jeera on a chakla - belan & add to the bhei mix. Mix crushed seeds of 1 illaichi also. Keep aside.
5. Soak kesar in a few drops warm water for 5 minutes. Mix with paneer to give it a yellow colour. Alternately, yellow colour may be added. Mix salt & pepper to the paneer. Add crushed seeds of 1 illaichi. Mix well.

Make small, marble sized balls of the paneer.

6. Make 4 big balls of bhein mixture. Flatten each ball. Put a small ball of paneer. Cover with bhei mixture to form the outer coating. Deep fry to a golden brown colour. Keep aside.

7. To prepare gravy, grind onions, ginger, garlic & tomatoes to a paste in a grinder. Heat oil. Add the above paste. Cook till dry.

8. Add crushed jeera, garam masala, red chilli pd., amchoor and laung. Cook for ½ minute. Cook stirring, till oil separates.

9. Add enough hot water (1½ cups approx.) to get a gravy. Add salt. Cook for 5-7 minutes on low flame. Add crushed seeds of 3 chhoti illaichi.

10. Boil gravy. Simmer on low flame for 4-5 minutes. Remove from fire.

11. To serve, cut koftas carefully into two halves and heat koftas in the oven. Heat the gravy separately. Pour the hot gravy in a dish. Arrange hot koftas over it. Garnish with a small rose made from tomato peel.

Note : When you purchase kamal kakri, see that they are closed on both ends. This prevents the dirt from going inside the vegetable.

Stir Fried Paneer : page 108

MAKHANI TOMATO PANEER

— Serves 6 —

½ kg (8 medium) tomatoes - chopped
4 laung (cloves)
¼ cup butter
1½ tsp sugar
salt to taste
½ tsp red chilli powder, ½ tsp garam masala
a few dhania (fresh coriander) leaves - chopped
200 gm paneer - cut into small cubes
1 " piece ginger - crushed to a paste on a chakla-belan

1. Cook chopped tomatoes, laung & ½ cup water, together in a pan, on low flame, till tender. Blend in a mixer. Strain to get tomato puree.
2. Mix sugar, salt, red chilli powder, butter & ginger paste with tomato puree. Cook for 5 minutes on low flame. Add pieces of paneer, garam masala & coriander leaves. Cook for a few minutes. Serve.

Nargasi Kofta : page 50

Basil Tomato Paneer

Picture on back cover

— Serves 4-5 —

300 gm paneer
4 large tomatoes - blanched, peeled & pureed
3 tbsp oil, 1 large onion - chopped finely
4-6 laung (cloves) - crushed
5-6 saboot kali mirch (peppercorns) - crushed coarsely

MARINADE

1½ cups curd - beat well till smooth, 2 tsp cornflour
a few basil leaves - finely chopped (2 tbsp), See note
1½-2 tsp salt, ¾ tsp red chilli powder

OTHER INGREDIENTS

2-3 tsp tomato ketchup, 1 tsp butter
1 tsp tandoori masala

1. Cut paneer into 1" pieces.
2. Mix all ingredients of the marinade and marinate the paneer it.
3. Blanch the tomatoes in boiling hot water for a few minutes. Remove skin and grind to a puree in the blender.
4. In a pan heat oil. Add the onions and laung. Stir fry for a few minutes till the onions turn light brown.
5. Add the prepared tomato puree, tomato ketchup, butter and tandoori masala. Cook for 5-7 minutes till absolutely dry. Remove from fire and let it cool. Keep aside till serving time.
6. At serving time, add the marinated paneer with all the curd to the tomato-onion masala. Cook on low heat for a few minutes till you get the desired gravy. Do not over cook. (The curd might curdle if the heat is too high or if the gravy is kept for too long on fire.)
7. Transfer to a serving dish. Sprinkle with crushed peppercorns. Garnish with chopped basil leaves.

Note: If fresh basil is not available, use 1 tbsp chopped tulsi leaves.

PANEER KHOYA MAKHAANA

— Serves 4 —

10-15 cashew nuts
100 gms paneer
100 gms khoya (dried whole milk)
1 cup makhaanas (puffed lotus seeds)
3 tomatoes pureed
2 big onions
1" piece ginger
2 green chillies
1 tbsp chopped fresh dhania (coriander leaves)
1 tbsp khus-khus (poppy seeds)
1 tsp dhania (coriander) pd.
½ tsp red chilli pd.
½ tsp garam masala (mixed spices)
salt to taste
1 tbsp kishmish (raisins)

1. Fry paneer, kaju & makhanas to a golden brown colour, all in separate batches.
2. Grind onions, ginger, chillies & coriander leaves with little water in a grinder.
3. Soak khus-khus for 10-15 minutes & grind to a smooth paste.
4. Heat 4 tbsp oil. Add the onions-ginger paste. Cook on low heat till oil separates.
5. Add the khus-khus paste. Cook for 1-2 minutes.
6. Add tomatoes pureed in a grinder. Cook till oil separates.
7. Add dhania pd., red chilli pd. and garam masala.
8. Grate khoya. Add khoya & mix well for 1 minute.
9. Add paneer, kaju and makhaanas. Mix well.
10. Add kishmish.
11. Add enough water to get a thick gravy. Boil.
12. Cook covered till makhaanas turn soft.
13. Serve hot, garnished with a little grated khoya and kaju.

CHATPATA RASSEDAR PANEER

— Serves 4 —

3/4 cup besan ka moongra
150 gms paneer - cut into 1½ " cubes

GRAVY
2 onions - grated
½ " piece ginger - grated
2 tomatoes - chopped
2 green chillies
3 cups hot water
½ tsp haldi
1 tsp dhania (coriander)powder
1 tsp red chilli pd.
½ tsp garam masala
½ tsp amchoor (dried mango pd)
1 tsp salt - to taste

1. Cut paneer into ½ " thick slices. Then cut into 1½ " squares. Deep fry paneer pieces to a golden brown colour & keep aside.
2. Heat 4 tbsp oil in a karahi. Add grated onions & ginger. Cook on low flame till onions turn golden & oil separates.
3. Add chopped tomatoes & green chillies. Stir till tomatoes leave oil and are completely mashed.
4. Add dhania pd, red chilli powder haldi, amchoor & garam masala. Cook for 1 minute.
5. Add boiling hot water to get a thick gravy. Simmer on low fire for 10 minutes. Add salt.
6. Add moongras & fried paneer. Keep on fire for 5-7 minutes.
7. Serve hot with rice.

Note: Moongras are big spicy besan ki pakodis available at namkeen shops.

KESARI PANEER

— Serves 4 —

200 gms paneer - cut into ½ " cubes

GRAVY

4-5 tbsp oil
2 large onions - very finely chopped
1" piece ginger
3-4 flakes garlic
¼ cup cashewnuts
1 tbsp desiccated or grated fresh coconut
1 cup curd
1 tsp garam masala
1 tsp red chilli powder
few strands of kesar (saffron)
½ cup milk
1½ tsp salt - to taste
½ cup (100 gm) fresh cream

1. Grind grated coconut & cashew nuts to a paste with a little water.
2. Grind ginger & garlic to a paste.
3. Soak kesar in 1 tbsp water for 5 minutes & dissolve by rubbing with the fingers.
4. Heat oil. Add **very finely** chopped onions & ginger-garlic paste. Cook till light brown.
5. Add garam masala, coconut & cashewnut paste. Cook for 1 minute.
6. Add beaten curd gradually. Cook on low flame till oil separates.
7. Add salt & dissolved kesar.
8. Add enough milk to get a thick whitish gravy. Boil. Simmer for 5-7 minutes.
9. Add paneer pieces. Keep on fire for 3-4 minutes. Add cream. Remove from fire.
10. Garnish with a few strands of kesar soaked in warm water and swirl a little cream with a teaspoon.

Kaaju Paneer Masala

— Serves 4 —

½ cup kaju
150 gm paneer

GRAVY

3 onions - sliced finely
3 tomatoes - chopped
3 flakes garlic - chopped (optional)
1" piece ginger - chopped
3 tsp magaz - tarbooz ke beej (watermelon seeds)
1 tsp khus khus (poppy seeds)
1 tsp salt
½ tsp red chilli pd
½ tsp garam masala
½ cup milk

1. Cut paneer into finger shaped long pieces. Cut each piece further into

smaller pieces of ½" length - (the size of kaju).

2. Fry paneer to a golden colour. Remove from oil. In the same oil fry kajus to a golden colour. Remove from oil. Keep aside.
3. Deep fry onions till golden brown in colour. Cool. Grind to a paste.
4. Mix tomatoes, garlic, ginger with 1 cup water in a small pan. Boil. Keep covered on low flame for 15 minutes till the tomatoes turn soft. Remove from fire. Cool. Grind to a puree. Keep puree aside.
5. Soak magaz & khus khus in ¼ cup water for 10 minutes. Grind to a paste. If the quantity is too little for grinding in an electric grinder, add 2-3 tbsp of the above onion paste.
6. Heat 2 tbsp oil. Add onion paste. Fry till golden brown.
7. Add red chilli pd. Add khus khus paste. Mix for a few seconds.
8. Add tomato puree. Cook for 5-7 minutes till oil separates.
9. Add milk gradually, stirring continuously for 3-4 minutes on low flame.
10. Add garam masala & salt to taste. Add enough hot water to get a thick gravy. Boil. Keep simmering on low flame for 10-12 minutes.
11. Add the fried paneer and kaju. Give one boil. Simmer on low flame for 3-4 minutes till the paneer is heated through & turns soft. Serve.

ⱱADIYAN WAALA ⱱANEER

— Serves 4 —

2 Amritsari Vadis
250 gms paneer

GRAVY
1 big onion - grated
3 tomatoes - chopped
1" piece ginger - crushed to a paste
½ tsp red chilli pd
¼ tsp haldi
1 tsp dhania pd
½ tsp garam masala
a pinch of amchoor (dried mango pd.)
salt to taste

1. Fry vadis in 5-6 tbsp oil in a karahi on low flame. Keep turning the vadis till they are evenly browned all over. Keep aside.
2. Deep fry the paneer pieces to a golden colour & keep aside.
3. To prepare the gravy, heat 3-4 tbsp oil. Add onions & ginger & cook on low flame till onion turns golden brown and the oil separates.
4. Add tomatoes. Cook for 10-15 minutes till the tomatoes get mashed & oil separates.
5. Add dhania pd., garam masala, red chilli powder, amchoor & haldi. Add fried vadi. Cook for 1 minute.
6. Add enough hot water to get a thin curry. Add salt to taste. Boil. Keep curry on low flame for 7-8 minutes.
7. Add paneer. Keep curry on fire for 3-4 minutes.
8. Serve hot with rice.

Note : Vadis are spicy dried lentil cakes.

Kali Mirch Paneer Tukdi

Picture on inside front cover

— Serves 4 —

200 gms paneer - cut into ¼" thick slices
1 tsp saboot kali mirch (peppercorns) - crushed roughly
2 tsp butter

GRAVY

3 tbsp oil or ghee
¼ tsp ajwain
2-3 flakes garlic - crushed
½ onion - chopped
½ capsicum - chopped
½ tsp red chilli powder, ½ tsp salt, or to taste
½ tsp garam masala, 1 tsp dhania powder
½ cup ready made tomato puree
1-2 tsp tomato ketchup
½ cup water mixed with 1 tsp cornflour

1. Spread softened butter on both sides of paneer slices.
2. Sprinkle half of the crushed peppercorns on the paneer slices and press well to embed them into the slices. Turn slices & repeat. Cut each piece into 2 triangles.
3. For the gravy, heat oil. Add ajwain. Wait for ½ minute.
4. Add garlic. Let garlic change colour.
5. Add onion. Stir till transparent on low flame for 1 minute.
6. Add masalas - garam masala, dhania powder, red chilli powder and salt. Mix well for ½ minute. Add capsicum.
7. Add tomato puree. Cook till dry, for about 2-3 minutes.
8. Add water & cornflour. Add tomato ketchup. Simmer on low heat for 5 minutes till slightly thick. Keep aside.
9. To serve, heat a non stick tawa or an oven. Brown paneer pieces on the pan or on the hot grill of the oven. Cook till well heated and light brown on both sides.
10. Heat gravy, put some at the base of the dish. Arrange the pieces of paneer on top. Sprinkle some gravy on the paneer if desired.

GOAN CHEESE-PEA CURRY

PASTE

½ fresh coconut - grated
10 dry red chillies
2 tsp saboot dhania (coriander seeds)
2 onions
2 tsp khus-khus (poppy seeds)
3 sticks dalchini (cinnamon); 3 laung (cloves)
3 saboot kali mirch (pepper corns)
10 flakes garlic
4 tsp oil

OTHER INGREDIENTS

250 gms paneer - cut into 1 " pieces
6 tomatoes - cut into big pieces
1½ cups shelled peas - boiled

Paneer Dil Bahaar : page 110

4 tbsp oil
salt to taste
½ tsp sugar, ½ tsp garam masala
¼ cup cream or fresh malai (milk topping)

1. Put 2 tsp of oil in a small karahi and fry the dalchini, khus-khus, laung, saboot kali mirch, saboot dhania and red chillies for a few minutes on low flame, till khus khus turns brown. Remove from karahi.
2. Put the onions straight on the gas until they become black. Cool. Remove the top skin. Chop onions.
3. Put 2 tsp oil in the same karahi and fry the grated coconut for 1 minute.
4. Mix all the fried ingredients of step 1, chopped onion, fried coconut and garlic together and grind to a smooth paste with a little water.
5. Boil tomatoes & 4 cups water in a pan. Cook covered, for 5-7 minutes till tomatoes turn soft. Blend in a mixer. Strain to get tomato puree.
6. Heat 4 tbsp oil in a karahi. Add the paste, tomato puree, sugar and salt. Boil. Cook for 10 minutes on low flame. Add paneer, garam masala, cream and boiled peas. Simmer on low flame for 4-5 minutes. Serve.

Achaari Paneer : page 94

SAFED MUGHLAI PANEER

— Serves 4 —

200 gms paneer - cut into ½" cubes
1 onion - grated
1 tbsp khus khus (poppy seeds)
1 tbsp kaju
1 tbsp magaz (water melon seeds)
4 tbsp curd
1 cup (200gm) fresh cream
1½ tbsp desi ghee or butter
¾ tsp garam masala
¾ tsp red chilli powder
¾ tsp salt or to taste
2 chhoti illaichi (green cardamom) - crushed to a powder

1. Soak khus khus, kaju and magaz in ¼ cup water for 10 minutes. Grind to a very fine paste.
2. Beat curd till very smooth.
3. Heat ghee. Add grated onion. Cook on low flame till it turns transparent and ghee separates. Do not let it turn brown by keeping on high flame.
4. Add kaju - khus paste. Cook for 2 minutes on low flame.
5. Gradually, add well beaten curd, stirring continuously. Cook for 5-7 minutes, stirring continuously on low flame.
6. Add garam masala, red chilli pd. & salt.
7. Add cream. Stir. Add paneer cubes. Mix well. Add a little milk if you want to thin down the gravy.
8. At the time of serving, add powdered chhoti illaichi and heat till paneer turns soft.
9. Serve garnished with a swirl of cream and a small stalk of fresh coriander leaves arranged on any side of the dish.

PANEER IN CORIANDER GARLICE SAUCE

-- Serves 4 --

200 gm paneer - cut into 1" cubes
3 dry red chillies - broken into bits
½ pod garlic - crushed to a paste
6 tbsp ready made tomato pure (kissan or Godrej)
OR
4 tomatoes
1½ tsp cornflour dissolved in 1 cup water
½ tsp sugar
½ tsp pepper
2 tbsp oil
1 tsp salt or to taste
1 tbsp tomato ketchup
¼ cup chopped fresh coriander (hara dhania)
2 green chillies - cut into thin long pieces

1. If fresh tomatoes are being used, put them whole in boiling water for 2-3 minutes. Remove from water. Put in a mixer and grind to a puree. Strain the puree to make it smooth. Keep tomato puree aside.
2. Heat 2 tbsp oil. Reduce flame. Add dried red chillies broken into bits.
3. Immediately add garlic paste. Cook for 1 minute on low flame. Add chopped coriander.
4. Add tomato puree.
5. Add salt, pepper & sugar. Cook for 1-2 minutes.
6. Add cornflour dissolved in water, stirring continuously. Boil. Cook on low flame till thick. Add tomato ketchup.
7. Add 1/2" cubes of paneer. Mix well. Cook on low flame for 2-3 minutes.
8. Serve, garnished with slit green chillies.

BENARSI BHARVAAN ALOO

— Serves 4 —

4 large potatoes
2 tbsp maida (plain flour)
oil for frying

FILLING
100 gms paneer
1 small onion - finely chopped
½ cup boiled peas
2 tsp broken kaju (cashewnuts)
1 tsp kishmish (raisins)
1 green chilli - chopped finely
salt to taste

GRAVY
4 tbsp oil
2 onions

½ " piece ginger
¼ tsp haldi (turmeric pd.)
½ tsp garam masala (mixed spices)
½ tsp red chilli pd.
1 tsp dhania (coriander) powder
¼ cup beaten curd
2 tomatoes
50 gm khoya (dried whole milk)
salt to taste

1. To prepare the potatoes, peel and wash potatoes. Prick with a fork. Cut into two pieces.
2. Scoop out the inner portion.
3. Keep the potatoes in salted water.
4. Prepare a thick maida paste with 2-3 tbsp water.
5. To prepare the filling, heat oil. Add onion and green chilli. Cook till onion turns light pink.
6. Add boiled peas, kaju & kishmish. Cook for 1 minute.

7. Add crumbled paneer and salt. Cook for a few seconds. Remove from fire and cool. Keep filling aside.
8. Dry the cut potatoes.
9. Fill the potatoes with the prepared filling.
10. Join the two halves with maida paste and tooth picks.
11. Deep fry the prepared potatoes in medium hot oil. Keep aside.
12. To prepare the gravy, grind onions & ginger.
13. Grind tomatoes separately.
14. Cook onion paste in oil, on low heat till light brown.
15. Add haldi, dhania pd, and red chilli pd.
16. Add tomatoes and curd and cook till oil separates.
17. Slow down the fire and mix in the khoya. Cook for a few seconds.
18. Add salt to taste.
19. Add the fried potatoes and enough water to get a thick gravy.
20. Cook covered till the potatoes are tender. Serve.

Sukhe or Dry Preparations

≈

Paneer Kadhai Waala

— Serves 4 —

200 gms paneer - cut into 1" cubes
4 onions - cut into rings
1 capsicum - cut into rings
2" long, piece of ginger - grated
6-7 flakes garlic - crushed
3 tbsp ready made tomato puree (Godrej)
1 cup thick curd
1 tsp salt
2 pinches sugar
5 tbsp oil

KADHAI MASALA
1½ tsp saboot dhania (coriander seeds)
3 dry red chillies
a pinch of methi daana (fenugreek seeds)

4-5 saboot kali mirch (pepper corns)
1 tsp jeera (cumin seeds)

1. Roast saboot dhania, jeera, red chillies, methi daana & saboot kali mirch on a tawa, on low flame for 4-5 minutes. Do not let the seeds turn brown. Cool & grind to a powder in an electric grinder or on the chakla - belan.
2. Heat 3 tbsp oil in a kadhai. Add onions & cook till brown. Add capsicum. Stir fry for 2 minutes. Remove from kadhai & keep aside.
3. Heat 2 tbsp oil in the kadhai. Add crushed garlic. Cook till light brown.
4. Add powdered kadhai masala. Cook for ½ minute.
5. Add grated ginger.
6. Add tomato puree. Cook for 1 minute.
7. Add curd gradually, stirring continuously. Cook for 5-7 minutes.
8. Crumble 4-5 pieces of paneer & mix with the masala.
9. Add rest of paneer pieces, fried onions & capsicums.
10. Add salt & 2 pinches of sugar. Mix well. Remove after a few seconds.
11. Serve hot.

KASAA PANEER

— Serves 4 —

200 gm paneer is required in all.

MASALA
2 onions
2 tomatoes
1" ginger piece
4 tbsp oil
1 tsp dhania (coriander) powder
1 tsp red chilli pd
1 tsp salt or to taste
1 tsp tandoori masala
4-5 laung (cloves) - crushed
5-6 tbsp chopped fresh dhania (coriander)
3/4 tsp bhuna jeera (roasted cumin seeds) pd.
a pinch of sugar

1. Thickly grate 50 gms (½ cup) paneer. Keep aside.
2. Cut the rest (150 gms) into small ½ " cubes.
3. Grind onion, tomatoes & ginger to a paste in a blender.
4. Heat 4 tbsp oil. Fry onion-tomato paste on low flame till almost dry.
5. Reduce flame & add dhania pd, red chilli pd. & salt. Cook for 5-7 minutes till oil separates and the masala is well fried.
6. Add just enough (3/4 cup) hot water to get a thick masala gravy. Boil. Keep on low flame for 5-6 minutes.
7. Add tandoori masala, laung & 3 tbsp of chopped dhania. Mix well.
8. Add grated and cubed paneer. Add bhuna jeera and a pinch of sugar. Stir gently on low flame for a few minutes till a thick masala is ready. Serve.

Stuffed Paneer

Picture on page 36

— Serves 6 —

½ kg paneer - block shaped
1 tbsp butter
½ tsp kala namak

FILLING
2 cups shelled peas
2 onions finely chopped
½ "ginger- finely chopped
2 tomatoes - finely chopped
3-4 tbsp oil
2 laung (cloves) - crushed
¼ tsp haldi (turmeric pd.)
¼ tsp red chilli
¼ tsp dhania powder, ¼ tsp garam masala
1 tsp salt or to taste

Pic. Page 36

1. Scoop out the block of paneer by making a hole from the longer side, leaving a border of 3/4 " all around. Do not dig till the bottom. Keep the bottom wall intact.
2. Keep the block aside. Crumble the scooped out paneer roughly.
3. Rub melted butter on the scooped out paneer block. Sprinkle kala namak on the paneer all over.
4. To prepare the filling, heat oil. Add onions & ginger. Cook till light brown.
5. Add tomatoes. Cook till tomatoes get mashed & oil separates.
6. Add haldi, red chilli pd, dhania and garam masala. Cook for ½ minute.
7. Add peas. Cover and cook till peas are done. Add salt & laung.
8. Mix in the crumbled paneer. Stir. Remove from fire.
9. Cool. Fill filling in the scooped out paneer block.
10. At serving time, place the paneer on a greased plate & grill the stuffed paneer block in the oven till slightly browned and the filling is heated properly.
12. To serve, place the whole block on a serving platter. Surround with the left over filling. Serve a flat spoon to cut into slices at the time of eating.

PANEER MUSHROOM

— Serves 4 —

½ packet (100 gms) fresh mushrooms
150 gms paneer - cut into ½ " cubes
2 simla mirchi (capsicums) - chopped
3 onions - cut into rings
1" piece ginger - chopped
3 tomatoes - chopped
¼ tsp haldi (turmeric pd.)
½ tsp red chilli pd
2 tsp dhania powder
½ tsp garam masala
¼ tsp amchoor
salt to taste - 3/4 tsp approx.
1 tej patta (bay leaf)
2 laung (cloves)- crushed
1 tsp tandoori masala

1. Wash mushrooms thoroughly and cut each into 4 pieces.
2. Heat 4 tbsp oil. Add onion rings & ginger and fry till onions turn light brown.
3. Add chopped tomatoes & cook for 3-4 minutes.
4. Add tej patta.
5. Add haldi, red chilli pd, dhania pd and garam masala. Cook for 1-2 minutes.
6. Add mushrooms. Stir for 1-2 minutes. Cover and cook for 8-10 minutes till mushrooms are done.
7. Add chopped capsicum. Cook, without covering for 3-4 minutes.
8. Add salt to taste. Add crushed laung, amchoor & tandoori masala.
9. Add paneer. Mix well. Stir fry for 1 minute on low flame. Serve hot.

Paneer Anaardaana

— Serves 4 —

250 gms paneer - cut into 1" pieces
3 tbsp oil
½ tsp sarson (mustard seeds)
1" ginger piece
6-7 flakes garlic - optional
1 tsp dhania (coriander) powder
½ tsp haldi (turmeric pd.)
¼ tsp black pepper powder
½ tsp red chilli powder
2 tomatoes - chopped finely
1 green chilli - chopped
2 tbsp anaardaana (pomegranate seeds)- powdered
½ tsp lemon juice - optional
½ tsp salt - to taste

1. Crush ginger & garlic to a paste on a chakla-belan.
2. Heat oil. Add sarson.
3. When sarson splutters, add the ginger-garlic paste. Fry paste for ½ minute.
4. Add dhania pd, haldi, black pepper powder, red chilli powder. Cook for ½ minute.
5. Add chopped tomatoes, anaardaana & salt. Cook for 2-3 minutes.
6. Add the paneer pieces. Stir gently.
7. Add lemon juice if desired. Serve.

BAINGAN BEMISAAL

— Serves 4 —

2 round baingans (brinjals)
8 tbsp besan (gram flour)
2 green chillies
salt, red chillies, garam masala (mixed spices) to taste
a pinch of amchoor (dried mango pd)

FILLING
2 onions - finely chopped
250 gms unshelled peas
1 big carrot - finely chopped
¼ " piece ginger - finely cut
250 gms paneer - roughly mashed (crumbled)
salt, red chilli powder and garam masala (mixed spices) to taste
2 tbsp oil

1. Boil whole brinjals in water, in a covered pan for 10-15 minutes until they feel soft when a knife is inserted through them.
2. Cool. Cut them lengthwise into two, keeping the stem intact in both the pieces. Scoop out the pulp, leaving a border of ½" all round. Keep aside.
3. To prepare the filling, heat oil. Add onions and cook till light brown.
4. Add shelled peas and carrots and cook till tender. Add paneer.
5. Add ginger, salt and other spices to taste. Cook for 1-2 minutes. Keep filling aside.
6. In a separte bowl mix besan, green chillies, salt and spices with enough water to form a thick batter of coating consistency.
7. Fill brinjals with filling. Press the filling well. Keep aside.
8. At the time of serving, dip the filled brinjals in batter and shallow fry in hot oil in a frying pan.

ACHAARI PANEER

Picture on page 72

— Serves 8 —

300 gms paneer
2 tsp saunf (aniseeds)
1 tsp sarson (mustard seeds)
a pinch of methi daana (fenugreek seeds)
½ tsp kalonji (onion seeds)
1 tsp jeera (cumin seeds)
5-6 flakes garlic - crushed to a paste (optional)
1 " piece ginger - crushed to a paste
½ cup curd
4 tbsp oil
3 onions - chopped finely
3-4 green chillies - chopped
1 tsp haldi (turmeric) pd.
1½ tsp amchoor (dried mango pd.)

Pic page 72

2-3 slit green chillies
1 tsp salt or to taste

1. Cut paneer into rectangular pieces.
2. Collect all seeds - saunf, sarson, methi dana, kalonji and jeera together.
3. Crush garlic and ginger roughly on a chakla-belan and keep aside.
4. Heat oil. Add the collected seeds together to the hot oil. Let them crackle for 1 minute.
5. Add onions and chopped green chillies. Cook till onions turn golden brown.
6. Add haldi and crushed garlic-ginger paste. Cook for ½ minute.
7. Beat curd with a spoon till smooth. Add gradually and keep stirring. Add amchoor and ½ tsp salt. Cook till the curd dries up a little.
8. At the time of serving, add the paneer cubes and slit green chillies. Sprinkle ½ tsp salt and ½ tsp red chilli powder on the paneer. Stir for 1-2 minutes on low flame. Serve hot.

LACHHA PANEER

— Serves 4 —

2 onions - cut into fine rings (lachhe)
2 capsicums - cut into fine rings
2 tomatoes - cut into slices
1 tbsp ginger - shredded
1 tsp lemon juice
200 gms paneer - cut into small cubes
3 tbsp oil
1 tsp salt or to taste
1 tsp dhania (coriander) pd
½ tsp red chilli pd
1/3 cup cream or well beaten malai
½ tsp garam masala

WET PASTE
1 green chilli

1" piece ginger
1 tbsp chopped coriander
1 tsp jeera (cumin seeds)
3-4 saboot kali mirch (pepper corns)

1. Cut capsicum, onion & tomato into rings. Remove pulp of tomatoes.
2. Grind all ingredients of the wet paste together.
3. Heat oil. Add onion rings. Cook till brown.
4. Add the ground paste. Cook for 1 minute. Add shredded ginger.
5. Add capsicum. Cook for 1 minute.
6. Add salt, dhania pd, garam masala and red chilli pd. Mix well. Add tomatoes & paneer.
7. Add 1/3 cup cream or malai. Cook for 1 minute.
8. Sprinkle lemon juice. Transfer the hot vegetable to a serving dish.
9. Garnish by finely grating some paneer directly over the vegetables in the serving dish.

Benaarsi Paneer

— Serves 4 —

250 gm paneer
3-4 green chillies
3-4 tbsp chopped coriander
1 tsp jeera (cumin seeds)
½ tsp salt
1" piece ginger
3 onions - finely chopped
2 tbsp oil
¼ tsp haldi (turmeric pd.)
½ cup beaten curd
¼ cup malai (cream) - optional
oil for frying

BATTER
¼ cup maida

1/3 cup water
½ tsp salt
½ tsp red chilli pd.
½ tsp garam masala

1. Cut paneer into ½ thick slices. Cut slices into 1" squares.
2. Grind green chillies, coriander, jeera, ½ tsp salt, and ginger to a paste.
3. Slit paneer pieces almost till the end, keeping the end part intact.
4. Rub the coriander paste over and inside the slits of paneer pieces.
5. Mix all ingredients of the batter together to get a batter of thin coating consistency.
6. Dip the stuffed paneer pieces in batter & deep fry in hot oil to a light cream (whitish) colour. Keep the fried paneer pieces aside.
7. Heat oil. Add chopped onions. Cook till transparent. Add haldi powder and ½ tsp salt. Cook for 1 minute.
8. Add curd and fresh malai. Mix. Add fried paneer pieces. Toss for a few minutes till slightly dry.
9. Serve hot.

Amritsari Paneer

— Serves 4 —

250 gm paneer
2" piece ginger (1 tbsp fresh paste)
10-12 flakes garlic (1 tbsp paste)
1 tsp ajwain
1 tsp red chilli powder
½ tsp haldi
½ tsp pepper powder
3-4 tbsp heaped besan
few drops orange red colour
3/4 tsp salt - to taste
oil for deep frying

ONION RINGS
2 onions - cut into fine rings
2-3 tbsp beasan
juice of 1 lemon
½ tsp salt
½ tsp red chilli powder

1. Cut paneer block into ½ " thick slices. Cut into 1" squares.
2. Grind ginger & garlic to a paste.
3. Mix ajwain, salt, red chilli pd, haldi and pepper powder with the ginger-garlic paste. Add orange red colour.
4. Rub 1 tbsp paste on the onion rings and the rest of the paste on the paneer pieces. Keep aside to marinate.
5. At serving time, heat oil for frying. Sprinkle besan on onion and paneer. Mix lightly.
6. Deep fry paneer till crisp.
7. Deep fry the onion rings also.

TANDOORI CHAAT

Picture on cover

— Serves 4 —

2 capsicums - deseeded and cut into 1½" pieces (preferably 1 green & 1 red capsicum)

200 gm paneer - cut into 1" cubes (8 pieces)

2 small onions - each cut into 4 pieces

4 fresh pineapple slices - each cut into 4 pieces (see note)

2 tomatoes - each cut into 4 pieces and pulp removed

1 tsp garam masala

2 tbsp lemon juice

1 tbsp tandoori masala or barbecue masala

2 tbsp oil

1 tsp salt, or to taste

1½ tsp chaat masala

1. Mix all the vegetables, pineapple and paneer in a bowl.
2. Sprinkle all the ingredients on them. Mix well.
3. Grease the grill or wire rack of the oven or tandoor and first place the paneer, pineapple and onions only on the grill rack. Grill for about 15 minutes, till the edges start to change colour.
4. After the paneer is almost done, put the capsicum and tomatoes also on the wire rack with the paneer etc. Grill for 10 minutes.
5. Remove from the oven straight to the serving plate. Sprinkle some chaat masala and lemon juice, if you like.

Note : If tinned pineapple is being used, grill it in the second batch with capsicum and tomatoes since it is already soft.

Zayekedar Paneer

PASTE

6-7 flakes garlic - optional
1" piece ginger
1 tsp saunf (aniseeds)
1 tsp jeera (cumin seeds)
3 dry red chillies
1 tsp dhania powder
1 stick dalchini (cinnamon)
3-4 laung (cloves)
3-4 saboot kali mirch (pepper corns)
seeds of 2 moti illaichi (brown cardamom)

VEGETABLES

2 onions - sliced
10-12 french beans
2 carrots

200 gm paneer - ½ " cubes
4-5 tbsp oil
1 tej patta (bay leaf)
juice of ½ lemon

1. Grind all ingredients of the paste together.
2. Thread french beans & scrape carrots. Put in salted boiling water for 3-4 minutes, till half-cooked. Remove from water. Cool. Chop into tiny pieces.
3. Heat oil. Add sliced onions. Cook till golden brown.
4. Add boiled vegetables and stir fry for 3-4 minutes.
5. Add the paste and tej patta. Cook for 1-2 minutes.
6. Add ¼ cup of hot water. Boil.
7. Add salt to taste & paneer cubes. Mix well. Sprinkle lemon juice. Mix. Serve.

POODINA PANEER

— Serves 4 —

½ bunch fresh poodina leaves - chopped
OR
¼ cup dried poodina
3 onions - sliced finely
250 gms paneer
¼ tsp haldi (turmeric pd.)
3/4 tsp red chilli pd.
3/4 tsp garam masala
2 tomato - chopped without pulp
salt to taste
4 tbsp oil

1. Cut tomatoes into 4 big pieces. Removing the pulp, chop into tiny pieces. Keep pulp aside.
2. Cut paneer into ½ " cubes.
3. Heat oil. Add onions. Cook till light brown. Add haldi, red chilli pd. & salt. Cook for ½ minute.
4. Add tomato pulp. Cook for 1-2 minutes till pulp is dry.
5. Add the paneer and finely chopped poodina & tomato pieces.
6. Add garam masala. Cook for 2 minutes. Remove from fire. Serve.

STIR FRIED PANEER

Picture on page 53

– Serves 4 –

200 gm paneer - cut into 1" cubes
2 spring onions with stalk - cut diagonally
75 gms (½ pack) mushrooms - halved
2 baby corns - optional - cut into 1" pieces
1 capsicum - cut into 3/4" pieces
2 tomatoes - finely chopped
3 tbsp butter
fewdrops of tobasco or capsico sauce
2 tbsp wocestershire sauce
salt to taste
¼ tsp pepper
¼ tsp red chilli powder

Pqc. Page 53

108

1. Cut the green stalks of spring onions diagonally into small pieces. Cut the white portion into thin slices.
2. Slit baby corns into two. Then cut into 1 " pieces.
3. Heat 2 tbsp butter in a non stick kadhai or pan. Add the white part of the spring onions. Saute for 1 minute till transparent.
3. Add tomatoes and cook for 3-4 minutes till they turn pulpy.
4. Add baby corn and mushrooms. Sprinkle some salt & pepper. saute for 1-2 minutes. Cover and cook on low flame for 3-4 minutes, till mushrooms get cooked.
5. Add capsicum & saute for 2 minutes, till slightly soft. Add the greens of the spring onions.
6. Add paneer cubes. Sprinkle worcester sauce and tobbasco sauce. Sprinkle some more salt & pepper if desired. Sprinkle chilli powder.
7. Stir fry for a few seconds & serve immediately.

Note : Vegetables can be cut & kept ready in advance but they should be stir fried (cooked) at the time of serving.

PANEER DIL BAHAAR

A quick way of preparing a different paneer dish. A little besan (gramflour) makes all the difference.

Picture on page 71

— Serves 6 —

250 gms paneer - cut into 1½" cubes
2 capsicums - cut into 1" pieces
2 small onions - cut into 1 " pieces
½ tsp red chilli powder
½ tsp garam masala
½ tsp salt
2-3 tsp besan (gram flour)
2 tsp kasoori methi (dried fenugreek leaves)
juice of ½ lemon

PASTE

1" ginger piece, 3-4 flakes garlic
2 dry, red chillies. 2 green chillies

OTHER INGREDIENTS TO BE ADDED TO THE PASTE

¼ tsp haldi
½ tsp ajwain (carom seeds)
2 tbsp malai or thick cream
1 tsp oil
½ tsp salt

1. Grind ginger, garlic, green and red chillies to a rough paste.
2. Add haldi, ajwain, malai or cream, oil & salt to the ginger-garlic paste.
3. Rub this paste all over on paneer pieces. Keep aside for 10 minutes.
4. Heat 2 tbsp oil. Add capsicum and onion pieces. Cook for 2 minutes on low flame. Add ½ tsp garam masala, ½ tsp red chilli powder and ½ tsp salt.
5. Add paneer pieces.
6. Add kasoori methi. Mix. Sprinkle 2-3 tsp besan. Cook on low flame, stirring continuously till paneer gets coated a little with besan.
7. Sprinkle some red chilli powder and lemon juice. Stir fry for 2 minutes on low flame. Serve hot.

PANEER IN KASOORI METHI

— Serves 4 —

1 packet (25 gms) kasoori methi (dried fenugreek leaves)
4 tbsp oil
4 tbsp fresh malai or cream
250 gms paneer - cut in tiny cubes
¼ tsp haldi
½ tsp red chilli pd.
salt to taste

1. Clean methi. Remove stalks. Wash in plenty of water. Soak in water for 1 hour atleast or preferably for some more time.
2. Fry paneer cubes to a light golden colour.
3. Heat oil. Squeeze the soaked methi and fry in oil for 4-5 minutes.
4. Add salt, haldi & chilli powder.
5. Add malai and cook some more.
6. Lastly add the lightly fried paneer. Mix well. Serve.

DHANIA-JEERA PANEER

— Serves 4—

200 gm paneer - cut into ½ "cubes
3-4 tbsp oil
1 tsp jeera (cumin seeds)
2 tsp dhania (coriander) pd
1 tsp amchoor (dried mango pd.)
1 tsp red chilli powder
1 tsp garam masala
1 tsp salt or to taste
a small bunch of fresh coriander - chopped along with stem
1 tsp chaat masala

1. Heat oil. Add jeera. When it turns golden, remove from fire.
2. Add dhania pd, amchoor, red chilli pd, garam masala & salt.
3. Return to fire. Add paneer & chopped dhania. Stir fry for few minutes.
4. Add chaat masala. Mix. Serve hot.

PANEER SIZZLER

– Serves 6 –

1½ cups shelled peas
200 gm (1 packet) fresh mushrooms - cut lengthways into thick slices
200 gm paneer - cut into1/2 " thick & 1½ " x 2" rectangular pieces
1 onion - chopped finely
3 tbsp butter
3-4 tbsp oil
salt to taste
a few freshly ground pepper corns (saboot kali mirch)
2 pinches of sugar
red chilli pd., garam masala & amchoor to taste
oil for shallow frying

1. Heat 1 tbsp butter. Add peas. Add salt, pepper & 2 pinches of sugar.
2. Cover & cook, sprinkling a few tbsp water occcassionally, till peas are done. Sprinkle some chilli pd., garam masala & amchoor. Keep aside.
3. Shallow fry the paneer cubes in 3-4 tbsp of hot oil on a tawa (griddle) till golden brown on all sides. Remove from oil. Sprinkle some salt, red chilli pd., garam masala, amchoor & freshly ground pepper on it.
4. Heat 2 tbsp of butter. Add chopped onion. Cook for 1 minute. Add sliced mushrooms. Add salt & pepper. Cook without covering on low flame for 2-3 minutes. Cover & cook for another 2-3 minutes till mushrooms are done. Sprinkle chilli pd., garam masala & amchoor.
5. Arrange a heap of peas in the centre of a flat oven proof platter or a low sided borosil dish.
6. Surround with mushroom slices.
7. Finally arrange a ring of paneer all round the mushrooms, slightly overlapping the mushrooms. Cover & keep aside.
8. To serve, keep the arranged sizzler in a hot oven for 4-5 minutes, till the paneer turns soft. Do not keep in the oven for more than a few minutes, because the paneer tends to become hard.

ᴇMBASSY ᴘANEER

– Serves 4 –

150 gms paneer - cut into tiny cubes
3 tbsp butter
½ " ginger piece - chopped finely
2 flakes crushed garlic - optional
2 onions - chopped finely
1 green chilli - chopped
1 tbsp maida (plain flour)
½ cup milk mixed with ¼ cup water
2 small tomatoes - chopped finely
1½ tsp salt
½ tsp pepper
½ tsp garam masala
½ tsp red chilli powder
1 tbsp tomato ketchup
3-4 tbsp chopped fresh coriander

1. Heat butter. Add onions, garlic, ginger and green chillies. Cook till onions turn transparent.
2. Add miada. Cook for half a minute.
3. Reduce flame and add milk & water mixture, stirring continuously. Keep stirring on low flame for 2 minutes till slightly thick.
4. Add tomatoes, salt, pepper and ketchup. Cook for 2-3 minutes.
5. Add cubes of paneer & fresh coriander. Mix gently for a few seconds.. Sprinkle garam masala & red chilli powder. Mix well. Serve hot.

RICE PANEER CASSEROLE

— Serves 4 —

½ cup rice basmati rice - soaked for 1 hour
2 laung (cloves) - crushed
1 tej patta (bay leaf)
½ tsp salt
¼ tsp each of red chilli pd, garam masala
2 tbsp oil

CABBAGE LAYER
1 cup shredded cabbage
1 cup thick curd
salt, pepper to taste
a pinch of powdered sugar
½ tsp lemon juice

PANEER LAYER
150 gms paneer - cut into 1" cubes
3 tomatoes - chopped
2 tbsp oil
½ tsp salt, pepper
1 dry red chilli
½ " piece ginger - crushed to a paste
1 tbsp tomato sauce

1. Hang curd in a thin muslin cloth for ½ hour. Beat well to make it smooth. Mix all ingredients of the cabbage layer with the curd. Keep aside.
2. Roast 1 red chilli directly on fire, turning, till it turns a little black. Soak in ½ cup water & keep aside. Mash after 15 minutes.
3. Heat 2 tbsp oil. Add dalchini. Add the chopped tomatoes and cook till oil separates.
4. Add red chilli along with the water & ginger paste. Cook for 1 minute.
5. Add salt, pepper & tomato sauce. Simmer on low flame for a few seconds. Keep this tomatoes sauce aside.

6. Deep fry paneer pieces & keep putting in hot water as you fry, to make the paneer soft.
7. To prepare rice, heat oil in a heavy bottomed pan.
8. Add tej patta & laung. Cook for ½ minute.
9. Drain the soaked rice & add to oil.
10. Add 1 cup water (double the amount of rice).
11. Add salt, garam masala & red chilli powder.
12. When the water boils, slow down the flame. Keep a tava under the pan of rice to reduce the heat further. Cook till water dries up and the rice is done.
13. To assemble all layers, take a transparent dish. Arrange a layer of rice. Press a little.
14. Spread cabbage mixture over it.
15. Mix the paneer with the prepared tomato sauce. Spread paneer with sauce over the cabbage.
16. Heat the dish at the time of serving.